WHAT IS A CHRISTIAN?

By

J. Todd Ferrier

1966

THE ORDER OF THE CROSS

10 De Vere Gardens, Kensington
London, W.8

IN THE NAME OF THE MASTER

I

CONTENTS

POEMS

THE PURPOSE

THE following words have been written as an exposition of the meaning of the Life and Teachings of the Blessed Master, to show what great, high and holy demands He made and now makes upon all who would follow Him in the Divine way of life. Such criticism of the Gospel Records as may be met with in the treatment of the question, has been made a necessity by the false view which they contain of the way the Master lived. For, as these Records are the only sources at the disposal of men and women in general whereby they may learn concerning the life of the Master, it is absolutely necessary to point out wherein the picture of Him is at fault, and how that fault arose.

It is quite true that these Records have come to be revered by the Western World, to be looked upon as things sacred in themselves whose very sacredness should shield them from criticism, and that the presentation of the Life and Teachings of the Master given in them should be accepted as a faithful portrayal. But to show wherein a picture is at fault is surely not to lack true reverence for the subject of the picture, but rather to manifest it in the earnest desire that the picture should be faithful. To point out what is lacking in any representation of the Blessed Master's Life and Teachings should not be interpreted as a lack of true reverence for Him, but rather the desire that the representation should be true, and worthy of Him.

If He were all that the Western World has claimed for Him, then He must not only have equalled in His purity, goodness and compassion all the Great Sages and Teachers of past ages, but He must also have transcended them. His ways in life must have been humane and pure beyond all question as the exposition of His goodness and compassion. The East as well as the West should be able to behold in such a presentation of Him, the humanity of a Buddha, the embodiment of BRAHM, the manifestation of Krishna. That the East fails to behold these things in the picture is most obvious; for the purity and humanity of the Master in the presentation given in the Gospels, are not those even of Buddha.

In occult philosophy it has been said that Christ can do anything. But whatever a Christ may do, He may not violate the Divine Nature within Him. He could never do anything contrary to the Divine Will, nor fail in the manifestation of the Divine Love.

That the Blessed Master lived a life crowned with the most beautiful exposition of purity, goodness and compassion, we know from a source which is more to be trusted than any records which are merely historical and traditional, however much such records may come to be revered through reverence for Him of whom they speak. That He gathered up into Himself those beautiful compassionate attributes associated with Buddha, the Sublime Vision of BRAHM, and the glorious manifestation of Krishna, we know. That He knew the meaning of Buddha, Krishna, and the BRAHM through the sublime realization within Himself, His true Life and Teachings made manifest. And had the New Testament Records contained a true representation of these, then readers of all lands would have found in Him the realization of that sublime Life for which all true Souls yearn.

If it should appear to be presumptuous on our part to claim access to a more trustworthy source of knowledge concerning the Life and Teachings of the Master than the present Gospel Records, yet it should be borne in mind that in every age in which any such claim had to be put forth in order that the truth should be told, it was always considered presumptuous. Even in the case of the Blessed Master Himself, it was so thought and affirmed by even the scholars of His day that He claimed to be the Son of GOD.

We grieve to be misunderstood and misrepresented; but the truth concerning the life of the Master has now to be told, and the marred picture of Him found in the Gospel Records replaced in the vision of all who would follow His way of life, by the true picture wherein the halo of His purity, goodness and compassion is seen to have been beautiful, luminous and glorious.

And if we are viewed as presumptuous in making such claims, yet shall we rejoice that it is in this sacred cause of the Master, in the restoration unto all Souls of the Vision so long lost, the Life He Himself lived and unto which He called all, the inner meaning of the Names which were afterwards given unto Him, the sublime purpose of His beautiful Christhood, and how the Western World has missed its way.

And unto that world which professes allegiance to the Christ, and unto the Churches which profess to interpret Him unto the Soul, would the writer present the true vision of the way the Master went, and along which He called all Souls to follow Him; and, also, all that it means in life to any one who would be a Christian.

The Source of the Soul's surest knowledge is that whence Prophets and Seers, in the days when the Heavens were open, derived their messages and visions, and Spiritual Vision and Angelic Communications were realities.

THE QUESTION

CAN one be a true disciple of the Blessed Master whilst continuing to eat the flesh of the Creatures?

Many will think the question not only to be unnecessary, but even to be impertinent. Men and women have long been accustomed to view the taking of the lives of the Creatures for food and raiment as one which was quite in keeping with true discipleship to the Blessed Master; for all the Churches, without exception, have looked upon it as a necessity in the economy of Nature that the Creatures should lay down their lives to sustain the bodies of men and women.[1] They have believed that the Divine Love had ordained that it should be done, and that to eat flesh was to obey the Divine mandate.

If, therefore, we were to answer the question in the negative, it would seem as if we were assuming the role of judge, and cutting off from allegiance to the Master the tens of thousands who do truly desire to follow Him, live His life, and take part in the Divine service.

Yet are we compelled to take up this position, however hard and unjust it may appear when judged of by those who only stand upon the outer

---

[1] We only know of two Churches in the whole Western World which make flesh-eating an obstacle to membership—one in Manchester and another in the U.S.A.

planes of life and perceive not that *all true life* must be lived from the innermost spheres, and that the outermost must be brought into perfect harmony with the innermost, otherwise the life will not be in true harmony. We are led to affirm that no one who takes the lives of the Creatures to minister unto their desires in any way can be a *true and intimate* follower and friend of the Master, because we know that the life which the Master lived and which He urged all who followed Him to live, was absolutely free from the evil of blood-guiltiness caused through sacrificing the Creatures upon the altars of the sense-life. One in Christhood could not violate the fundamental laws of the Divine Order, the laws of true compassion and pity. To have done so would have meant the abrogation of the beautiful Estate with all the Divine Heritage it implied. It would have been to contradict the very nature of the Christhood, and degrade His Divine Mission.

Men and women do not seem to understand the meaning of a Christhood; nor do the Churches appear to apprehend the significance of the life which it implied. They like to think that the Blessed Master was pure. Yet they imagine that He lived as other men lived in eating and drinking. They do not behold what is meant by the beautiful purity of the Master or they would at once see how impossible it was for Him to eat flesh or encourage others to eat it. They love to think that He was sublimely compassionate. Yet they can believe that He followed those ways of life whose paths run blood, that the blood of the Creatures slain in the abattoirs to meet the demands of the sense-life of thoughtless men and women, made no appeal to Him. And so they naturally think that one can be truly compassionate and at the same time eat the flesh of slain creatures; that one can know a Divine Pity and yet agree to their wholesale slaughter for food, and the imposition upon tens of thousands of others of tortures unnameable; that one may make of them mere goods and chattels of merchandise for men and women to buy and sell and get gain, irrespective of what is to become of them, and through it all retain the compassion which is said to have moved the Blessed Master towards all Souls.

It is indeed sad to think that men and women who should know the true meaning of following the Blessed Master could ever have had given to them such a view of the meaning of His wonderful ministry. And it is especially sad that within the Christian Churches where the true vision of His Christhood should surely have been known, a view of the meaning of the Master's Christhood prevails, which is a violation of all pity, the antithesis of compassion, and the abrogation of that profound and sublime experience implied in the wonderful Christhood to which He had attained.

SOME DISTINGUISHING FEATURES

THAT a follower of the Blessed Master may not eat flesh will be recognized when the meaning of the Master's life is understood. What was the purpose of that life? Was it not one of Redemption? What was the nature of the Redemption which He meant to accomplish? Was it not the restoration to man's life of the Divine purity, love and goodness? And how were these to be restored within man's spiritual system, unless the man was to be purified upon every sphere of experience, learn the profound and all-embracing nature of the Divine Love, and the universality of the Divine Goodness in its manifestations? And how could a man become pure whilst he defiled his body with the flesh of the sacrificed Creatures, his mind with the unlovely conduct of having the helpless slain to minister unto his low tastes, and his heart with the violation of the fundamental principles of all true compassion and pity? How could he come to know the Divine Love without first realizing its own tender reverence for *all life?* How could he know and understand the Divine Goodness unless he learnt to permit it to flow as a life-giving stream through his own life, expressing itself in gentleness, fellow-feeling, and spiritual kinship with all true forms of life?

That this view of Redemption to a true spiritual state is not that which the Churches believe in and teach, will be admitted by all who have learnt at the shrines of these Communities. For the Churches, though differing amongst themselves, nevertheless all date their origin and teaching from the Records which were supposed to have been written by those who knew the Master and understood what His Christhood meant. But in these Records the true Redeemed Life illustrated by the Master is so obscured that none can tell what it really was, except those unto whom it has been given to behold the erroneous presentation, to see the true picture, and to restore the long-lost vision of the Christhood. The Redemption to be accomplished by the Master is not presented in the Records as a life lifted up out of the influences of the evil conditions which prevail in the world, but rather as something to be accomplished by Him, quite apart from the upliftment of the Soul and its co-operation in the work.

It is presented as a mysterious work wrought on behalf of the Race, the true nature of which none may fully understand. And all the Sayings in which the Redemption is spoken of, have been made to relate to the personal Jesus, rather than to the Christhood which was made manifest through Him, consequently their mystic meanings were all changed, and their profound significations became lost. That happened to them which happened to the pure spiritual teachings in other ages. They were made material instead of spiritual in their meanings, and personal rather than universal in their relationships.

The Redemption was thus changed from being a Divine work within man, to that of a Divine work outside of him, and apart from him; from an inward experience whose influences touched the whole realm of man's life, to be only a work wrought on his behalf, by which the attitude of the Divine Love was changed towards him.

Such is the picture of the Redemption of the life presented in the Records upon which the Churches have built up their organizations and theories. And it is not difficult to understand how it has happened in the Western World where the religion of a Christhood is widely confessed, that the true Redeemed Life has not been understood by those who worship within the various Sanctuaries.

   .   .   .   .

What are those features which should distinguish a Christian from any who may not profess belief in Christ and the Christhood? Are they to be regarded as mere intellectual differences, the results of difference of birth and environment? Are they to be circumscribed by the assent of the mind to certain views held by the Churches, or the outward admiration of the Master and professed allegiance to Him such as the world gives to earthly potentates? Are they to find the fullness of their manifestation in the religious fervour and ecclesiastical devotion which are characteristics of all religions? Are not all these features to be found where no Christhood is professed, where the religious concepts and life are considered to be greatly inferior to those of the Christian? Indeed, in some of the Eastern religions there is a far higher conception of the sacredness of all life than may be found in the West. The principles underlying these religions inculcate humaneness in a way unknown within the Christian Churches. And the writings upon which these religions are founded lay stress upon true charity or love towards all the Creatures as one great essential to the right understanding of Divine Things and the attainment of the Divine Life.

Wherein then lie the distinguishing features of Christianity and of the man who would interpret Christianity in his life by being a Christian? Is it not in this, that Christianity gathers up into itself every good in all the other religions, giving to them a new and higher meaning, transcending them in its vision of the purpose of the Divine Love concerning this world and all its children (Human and Creature), and giving a very real meaning to the Soul in its Evolution, Fall, Redemption and Regeneration? And in gathering up all that is good in the other religions, it could not fail to make manifest a most beautiful love towards all Souls, a compassion immeasurable in its outflow unto all who are weak and defenceless, and a pity towards the Creatures tender and boundless. It could not fail to reveal wherever it was truly received, a life full of purity and goodness, a life whose every sphere was purified and which made manifest the Redeemed Life as the attainment of Redemption. It would not fail where the other religions had failed by simply setting forth the nature of the Redeemed Life (as in the case of Buddhism), and leaving man without a perfect embodiment of its meaning, but would give a most unmistakable manifestation of what the Redeemed Life was, so that all men might in beholding it know the nature of the life unto which they were called. And, as the crown of all other religions it would not fail to show forth the inner meaning of a Christhood, what it was in its nature, how it was to be attained, and in what sense it was the crown of the Redeemed Life; and it would illustrate all these things in a sublime interpretation given in manifestation through one who lived the Redeemed Life and was crowned with the Christhood Estate.

That the Life and Teachings of the Blessed Master transcended any manifestation in earlier times would have been known unto the whole Western World had the Records which purport to portray Him as He lived and taught, contained a true and faithful portrait. But these Records do not contain a true picture of Christ. For had they done so the path to Christhood would not have been hidden. The true way unto the Christhood Estate would have been obvious unto all who desired to enter upon it. The Redeemed Life with its *threefold path* would have been clear unto every reader. There would have been no room for doubt as to anything the Master meant when He called men and women to live the Redeemed Life. His Teachings concerning the way of the Redemption would not have been so obscure as they now are, and men and women would have known that true Redemption was a thing to be accomplished within them through the Soul and all its powers seeking to realize the Divine Way of Life, the way of purity, goodness and love.

But that these things are obscure must be evident to anyone who knows what the Redemption means. To them the Records must appear as remarkable and strange betrayers of the picture of Christhood, since they fail to direct the Soul to the threefold path of the Redeemed Life, and, instead, simply direct the mind to a personal allegiance to the Master as the true meaning of following Him.

THE PORTRAIT OF THE MASTER

WE have seen that the Records which profess to give a true portrait of the life of the Blessed Master fail in those things which some of the other great religions emphasised. The portrait is not that of a Christ, though the Master is so called in them. It is not even that of a Buddha; for there is no direct teaching concerning the relationship which exists between the Human and the Creature Kingdoms, and the attitude which the Christian must assume towards all the Creatures. Had the portrait been truly that of the Blessed Master as He was, then not only would the relationship of the Christian to the Creatures have been made clear, but it would have been also shown to have been an essential experience in the threefold path of the Soul seeking to follow the Christ. And had the Christhood been truly drawn by the writers of these Records, then all the world could by this time have come to the knowledge of the meaning of the beautiful Estate known as Christhood, and every earnest seeker who desired to understand the Divine Mysteries would have been able to follow the Teachings of the Master, arrive at the vision of the Divine Love within the Sanctuary of the Soul, and even come to know the Divine Wisdom through entering into the wonderful experiences expressed by the term Christhood. Then there would have been no need to inquire "What is a Christian?" so manifest would the answer have been. Christianity would have been a truly living force in the world; not as at present, but as it was meant to be. The astonishing ecclesiastical systems which have grown up in its name would have found no place; nor would the awful conflicts between the various sections have been known. For the whole world would have had the Holy Breath upon its spheres as the outcome of the beautiful lives through whom the Christhood was made manifest and the heavenly Wisdom interpreted. The awful burdens which are now crushing the lives of the toiling millions would have been unknown; for the conditions out of which they have grown would have been impossible. The shameful and unspeakable systems whose ramifications have penetrated the Churches, and whose whole influence is for evil, could have found no soil in which to grow. The blighting Drink Traffic with its holocaust of victims and its indescribable influences for degradation and woeful tragedy, would have found no men and women to support it, nor Churches to shelter those who sought to impose so infamous a wrong upon the children of the Great Love. The equally evil system represented by the abattoirs and shambles would have been unknown with all its cruel and shameful work; for the people would have loved purity in their ways, and humaneness would have adorned them as a beautiful garment. The Creatures would have been cared for and loved as the little spiritual children in the great Household of the FATHER-

Mother. The health of all the people would have been so different; for they would have known and followed the ways of health. The evil, cruel and inhuman work of vivisection, and all that it implies, would never have been conceived of by those who were the physicians and healers. Love between man and man would have triumphed. Compassion in man towards all the Creatures would have shone gloriously. Pity would have had a real dwelling-place and fullness of manifestation. The vision of the Redeemed Life would have led Souls to the realization of its purity, goodness and love. The vision of the Christhood would have led many into the vision of the Divine Love, and not a few into the vision of the Divine Wisdom which maketh all things clear unto the Soul.

The Records failed in things essential. The writers obscured the vision of Christhood. They misrepresented the Redemption, and gave a false picture of the sublime Master. Behold the Western World where they are believed!

THE THREEFOLD PATH

A CHRISTIAN is one who follows Christ where-soever He leadeth. He follows Him along the path which imposes upon all the desires and affections great self-denial in respect to their more outward manifestation. For that is the first path which the Soul must learn to tread. The man who would truly follow Christ must take up his cross and bear it along the road of *self-denial*. The sense-life must be chastened. It must be restrained in all its outgoings and purified in all its feelings. The outer spheres of experience must be made quite pure. Nothing must enter into the outer courts of the Temple which would defile them. The tastes must be brought into perfect harmony with the innermost desires of the Soul. "If any man would follow Me he must take up his cross and deny himself." "Following" was to be along the road of purification of all the senses. "If a man will not deny himself, he cannot be My disciple," showing clearly that such a purification was absolutely essential to true discipleship.

And wherein was man to deny himself were it not in those things which men and women in general seek after? What are those things most sought for by men and women? They are the things of the sense-life, the gratification of the sense desires, the eating of flesh and drinking of wine, and the pleasure which gratification of the senses gives.

These things a man must overcome if he would follow Christ. He must learn to deny himself every gratification of the sense-life wherein mere pleasure is sought. He must conquer the adversary on the outer spheres if he would attain to the glory of the inward Life. He must "go forth bearing his cross" through all the outward spheres of experience, however heavy that cross may become to him. He must cease ministering to his body except as to a precious vehicle through which he has to make manifest his inmost purposes, and he must nourish it upon the pure fruits of the Earth. If he would know the Christ, he must first learn to know Jesus. If he would follow the Christ he must first follow Jesus. When he has followed Jesus along the path which bringeth purification, then will he understand the true meaning of the Jesus-life. He will know that it is not a personal following of the Master, but a spiritual experience which leadeth the Soul upon all its spheres into a state of Redemption.

To be a Christian is, therefore, to be a man who knows the Redeemed Life.

When a man has accomplished the first step through self-denial and purification, then may he go on to know Christ. Having learnt the meaning of the Jesus-life he may seek for the meaning of the Christhood. But he is met on the way by the step which leadeth unto the Christhood path; it is the step which imposes upon the Soul renunciation of all things for the sake of Christ.

It is recorded in the Gospels that when the disciples were contending as to which of them should be first in the new kingdom, the Master affirmed that unless a man were prepared to forsake everything in this world—goods, estate, family traditions and ways, even those most closely related to him in the outer spheres—he could not know Christ.

This would appear at first sight as something contrary to the ways of a true and beautiful love. Yet when understood as the Master meant it, there is beheld a profound truth which all who would follow Christ must learn. When the Soul is following Christ along the second path it must needs learn that all outward things and relationships have only an outward and temporary value, and that their real value lies in their uses for truly spiritual ends. No other uses are recognized in the Heavens of the Divine Love. Nor can they be recognized by the Soul who would follow the Master. And so everything of the Earth in its outward spheres must be renounced as things which are to have no value in the Soul's just estimation of life. The love for them which is so characteristic a feature of the life of men and women to-day, is opposed to the true progress of the Soul, because it draws the Being earthwards to find satisfaction for its noblest longings in them. When, therefore, the Soul sets out to follow Christ, it must needs learn how to renounce all these things, so that in its following it may be hindered by none of them.

How often a Soul is hindered through its social and family ties from pressing forward in the path that leads to the Christ-life. Pride of birth and heritage, love of social position, desire to hold the things of the world as valuable possessions, longing to know success as the world accounts it, to have fame such as men and women seek, to keep the old friendship born from the earthly conditions—all these things have to be renounced. Their power over life has to be broken. The Being must be set free from the love of them that nothing may retard its progress in the path along which the Christ-vision draws it.

Thus is it that the experience comes to those who really love divine things, in which life is made hard for them, the path difficult, the renunciation great, when in the path they have to forsake the old ways and affections—friends, land, goods, heritage, prestige, with all the pleasures which these bring. They have not only to be pure in all their ways of life, but also spiritual in all their purposes; for the kingdom they seek is purely spiritual, and concerns itself only with spiritual things. And so we see what a profound meaning lies couched in the term Christian, and what it implies for the Soul who would be a Christian indeed.

Nor is that the full answer to the question: What is a Christian? Purity in all the spheres of life is absolutely essential. Renunciation of all earthly things and attachments is likewise a necessary experience. But in following Christ there is one more step to ascend which leads unto the realization of Christhood itself. It is to ascend the cross of absolute abandonment to the Divine Service. It is not only to know the crucifixion of the desires of the sense-life and the renunciation of the world for things spiritual and Divine, but it is also to go wheresoever the Spirit of the LORD directeth, and bear whatsoever burden of service HE may in HIS Holy Wisdom deem expedient to impose. It is not only to be pure in all the ways of our life, and spiritual in all its aims, but it is to have the beautiful spirit of true childhood unto the Divine Love, humble and obedient even unto the death of our most cherished hopes, willing to be even a seeming failure in the world of service, submissive to the Divine Will should that will demand that we should be crucified before the world by those who failed to understand us, and forsaken by all in whom we had trusted and loved.

The pathway of the Christian is not only one lit up with a great and glorious hope, and one full of the promise of a spiritual enrichment of the life, but it is also a pathway leading through the "Via Dolorosa" upward to "the Cross of Calvary" where the crosses of Self-denial and Renunciation meet in that yet fuller cross of perfect Self-surrender or Abandonment to the Divine Service.

"Are ye indeed able to drink of the cup of which I shall drink? and to be baptized with the baptism that I shall have?"

Thus did the Master inquire of two who would follow the Christ unto perfect realization of Christhood.

And they replied, "We are able."

The answer is now before us: Who would follow on to be a Christian?

WHITHER IT LEADS

WE have seen that the path of the Christian is threefold, that it embraces Self-denial, Self-sacrifice and Self-abandonment, and that only through the realization of these does the Soul become a Christian in very deed, one who knows Christ and has entered into Christhood.

We have beheld all that Self-denial implies; how it makes the life give up those things whose use is hurtful to the Creatures and the body, and degrading to mind and heart; how it demands that every sphere shall be pure, that the sense-life shall learn to be dumb until every sense becomes the avenue through which the Redeemed Life is made manifest.

We have seen how the path along which the Christian travels insists upon Renunciation as the next step, how the life must learn to give up all that it has, to sacrifice every earthly interest, to forsake all worldly estate and possessions as things to be valued and loved, to know by experience the meaning of Self-sacrifice when even the most sacred ties upon the outer spheres have to loosen their hold upon the life until the Soul even walks alone.

We have also seen that the way of Christ draws the Soul yet further from the ways of men and women when it impels it to walk through the "Via Dolorosa" and ascend the "Hill of Calvary" unto crucifixion of its most ardent hopes, however pure and beautiful they may have been; how in the hour of crucifixion the world's scorn may be poured upon the Soul, and the deep sorrow of desertion by all whom it has loved, break upon it. And now we have to look at the result unto the Soul of all these experiences, the kind of life by which it is crowned, the realizations which come to it, and the service unto which it is called. For to be a Christian is to be as a Christ.

The soul who has passed along that threefold path at last arrives at the state of spiritual experience known amongst the most ancient Hebrews (not the Jews) as Zion, and amongst the inner group of the Master's disciples as Christhood. It was said by the Hebrew Prophets and Seers to have been the ancient estate of Israel, those who had prevailed with GOD and had become HIS princes upon the Earth. And it was always unto the Holy City of Zion that Israel were counselled to return and come again to the vision of the Divine LORD within the Sanctuary. So the Soul who follows the threefold path is of the Redeemed of the LORD who return unto Zion, the Holy City of the LORD.

To arrive at that state is to attain unto the Vision of the Divine Presence within the Sanctuary of the Soul; and to reach that Vision is to be interiorly illumined from the Divine. It is to be baptized with the Sevenfold Spirit, the baptism of Christhood when the Soul is crowned "A Son of GOD". It is to be wreathed with the laurels of the conqueror, one who has overcome and risen to the Right Hand of the Majesty on High, by which is to be understood the rising up of the Soul into the blessed realization of the Divine Love, the Divine Wisdom, and the oneness of the One Divine Life.

To be a Christian, therefore, is to be a Soul who knows and lives the Redeemed Life, who understands and lives the life of Self-sacrifice, who sees and follows the Divine Will wheresoever it leadeth, until at last it is crowned with Christhood, and becomes one whose Lamp is kindled from the LORD, one whose Soul is illumined from the Divine, and who only needs to retire into the silence for communion to know from the Divine those Heavenly Things which no man can give nor the wisdom of the world impart.

THE LARGER ISSUES

IN the light of the things which we have written, things concerning the truth of which we have both seen and heard within spheres which are not adjacent now to this Earth, the real Spiritual World, the world of the Soul and the Divine Light, it will not be very difficult for us to also conceive of the true Church as to the life and ministry of its members. For the full answer to the question: "What is a Christian?" is likewise the answer to the question: "What is a Christian Church?" For the Church must be the fuller, because multiplied, manifestation of all that is implied in the term Christian.

The Christian Church should be Christian in its Fellowship, its Worship, its Communion, and its Ministry unto the world. It should be composed only of men and women who know and live the Redeemed Life, men and women who have sought to purify all their ways, who have had that vision which makes purity of life a necessity unto them and fills them with compassion for all Souls and pity unto all the Creatures.

They should be men and women who in their fellowship truly love the Brethren without any regard to their mere earthly estate, men and women of humble heart who desire to attain the spirit of the little child in all their ways.

They should be men and women whose fellowship would be as the breath of Heaven unto the Soul, because they know the purified life, have come into direct touch with heavenly things, have risen on to the Spiritual Heavens to behold the Angelic Life there and receive of the Angelic Wisdom from the Divine, who have themselves become recipients of Divine Illumination and true Mediums through whom the Divine communicates His love and Wisdom unto those Souls who are not grown sufficiently towards the Divine to enable them to receive these within themselves.

They should be men and women who are not only pure in all their ways and spiritual in all their aims, full of a love which is born from the Divine within them, and which manifests itself in profound compassion for all Souls, and unfailing pity unto all Creatures, but who also have within themselves the consciousness of the Divine Presence.

They should, therefore, be in this world the repositories of the Divine Presence, and be always conscious of it, and derive all their illumination and guidance through the consciousness of that Presence. When they worship it should be with "the open vision" which the consciousness of the Divine Presence within the Sanctuary of their Being gives them. The Spirit of the Fear or Divine Awe of the LORD should fill them and make even the earthly house of their fellowship a place whose gates are as doorways through which the breath of the Heavens is felt. It should be worship, indeed, in which all earthly things should pass out of the vision and be replaced with purely Spiritual and Divine things. The whole Being of each worshipper should be uplifted from the Earth into the clear air of "the heavenly places", to behold with open vision upon the Heavens the Glory of the LORD as that glory is broken unto them. Their communion should be with the Divine Love and HIS Saints, and the Angelic World should be a beautiful reality unto them. Upon them should sit the Tongues of cloven Fire, the signs of their inspiration and the testimony of their Christhood.

What a wealth of meaning is couched in the expression *A Christian Church!* And in the realization of that meaning, what wealth of spiritual riches and power is given for the accomplishment of the Redemption! In the manifestation of the life of such a community of Souls, what illumination would break upon the ways of life in the world to expose evil and error, and make clear the true path along which the Soul must needs walk if it would enter into the experience of the Redemption! How real would the Spiritual Heavens become unto every true seeker who desired the heavenly life, if the Church were thus Christian! The Ladder that was seen let down from the Heavens to rest upon the Earth, would no longer be a mere dream-story but a glorious reality; for the ministry of Angels would have become known and realized.

What the Soul in its life and ministry must become

if it would follow Christ, so the Christian Church *must* become. Great influences are sweeping over the whole Western World as the outcome of the Soul's awakening from its long spiritual sleep to seek for and find "the Treasure hid in the field" of its own history and regain once more "the Pearl of great price"—the Christhood Vision and Life.

There is a great spiritual upheaval. The foundations of the Earth are being shaken. Old positions are being changed, old ways of thought are being forsaken. The land-marks tell of the leaving of the old heritages and the seeking for and, in some cases, the entering into new lands with fairer life and heritage. The "beliefs" of men and women are passing from phase to phase, bringing the thoughtful and earnest nearer to the true path by which the glorious goal is to be won. The foundations of the Churches are also being moved. There is a shaking of the dry bones amid the desert of spiritual life, the breathing of a new vitality into institutions which have for ages been lifeless, the passing away of the old vision of things through the Soul seeking for something nobler, the craving after a living expression of Christianity rather than the ecclesiastical and priestly one.

As institutions the Churches are changing with the times. The claims of dogma and tradition by which they bound themselves and prevented their spiritual growth and enlightenment, are being broken. They are beginning to realize the needs of Humanity and to try and meet them, though they are yet far from understanding the true meaning of a Christian Church. They see how much society requires of purification in order to accomplish its Redemption, though they themselves are not yet in the path of Redeemed Life. Indeed, the true meaning of Redemption has not yet dawned upon them. There is no *open vision* with them yet, they see not the Divine path. They have not yet arrived at the meaning of purity, nor the knowledge of the nature of the Soul and the Oneness of all true life. They are still blinded by the gods of this world as at present constituted—Mammon whom they worship in many forms; Moloch unto whom they sacrifice the Creatures in unspeakable numbers; Beelzebub the lover of discord and strife, whose ways, alas! they have not yet ceased to follow.

But the Day of Redemption for them is also at hand. The Hand of God is upon them to make them purge their courts, cleanse their ways, and offer upon their altars pure oblations. The threefold veil, which has been thrown over them almost since the day of their foundation which was soon after the Blessed Master made manifest the Christhood, is being removed. The idolatry of worshipping the personal Jesus in place of the Divine FATHER-MOTHER is gradually ceasing throughout Christendom, for the Soul is being recalled to the true worship of the Ever Blessed ONE who makes HIM-SELF manifest within the Soul's Sanctuary. The veil which obscured the Divine Love through the exaltation of the personal Jesus as the object of worship, is now being taken away in order that the vision of the Ever Blessed ONE may break upon the Soul.

But the two other veils remain, though the day breaketh when they also must fall apart to let in the light of the Glory of the LORD, to show forth the true way of Love and the path of Redemption, the glory of the Redeemed Life and the diadem of Christhood. For the veil of blood is still over the Churches. They slay the Creatures in the name of the Divine Love to minister unto their unpurified tastes and desires, knowing not that it is the way of Moloch to make the little children (the Creatures) in the great Household of the FATHER-MOTHER pass through the fires of suffering and anguish; for such is the whole traffic in their lives. And until that veil is put away no vision of the Divine Love can break upon the Soul. For there must be purity in living, humaneness in feeling, compassion made manifest in unfailing pity.

And then the third veil must be put away, that veil by which not only the vision of the Divine Presence within the Sanctuary has been hidden, but also the Queen of Heaven, the feminine principle of the Soul, the Intuition. The Churches would never have gone wrong had not the Intuition of the Soul been veiled; indeed, they would never have been founded in the manner in which they were had not the gods of this world blinded the Intuition of those who laid their foundations. Moloch they have always sacrificed unto, as the Jews had done before them. Mammon soon found a place on their altars and claimed their reverence. And Beelzebub—the prince of darkness and the darkening one—from the beginning, obscured the Soul's Vision and drove out the Seer and the Prophet.

When the Churches have put away these three veils, then will they arrive at the right understanding of what is meant by a Christian Church as to its Life, Communion and Ministry. Then will they know the Redeemed Life and teach it. And they will understand Christ and make Him manifest in Christhood. Then will they know those things of which now they have but dim visions, and speak of the Divine Love and Wisdom as those who have realized them. In that day will the Heavens and the Earth be as one unto them, for they shall behold with open vision the life of that Spiritual World in which they have only in a vague way believed, and enter into the realization of those blessed Communions of Souls for which they now only falteringly hope.

THE PLAY OF REDEEMING FORCES

IF all the Churches in the Western World were truly Christian, what a wonderful World it would be! It would be a Christendom in very deed, a world of Souls who were seeking unto the finding of Christhood. How very different would be the policies of the various nations and the purposes of all the Communities. How changed the conditions of life would become within the Communities, how pure and beautiful even to transparency would the ways of men and women be.

It would be a world to make glad the life and fill the heart with unalloyed joy; for it would be a Redeemed World, and the life of its denizens would be the Redeemed Life. In it the things which make life sad and sorrowful would have no place, for the worshippers of Mammon, Moloch and Beelzebub would cease to inherit the land, and all the graven images of these world-gods would be thrown down. The cradle-song of the poor would never be sung, for there would be none who lacked nourishment. There would be no such fearful tragedies as are now written by so many lives, for all the evil pitfalls would be banished from the land. No longer would the sounds of strife and discord be heard in home, community or nation, for the things which bring peace and harmony would be established, and the Divine Love would reign in every life. The cries of anguish would no longer be heard breaking forth from the Creature Kingdom, for the prison-houses would be closed and the altars of sacrifice thrown down: such a world would know neither Abattoirs nor Physiological Laboratories, for all Souls would live upon the pure fruits of Nature and indulge in the flesh-pots of Egypt no more. The Social and National conditions would all be changed. The world's Princes would not be those who were simply born so of Blood, or of the Flesh, or of the Will of Man, but those who were Princes indeed, Israelites in whom there was no guile, Souls who had been crowned from the Divine as Sons of God, the Illumined Ones through whom the Divine was made manifest and interpreted. There would no more be Lords many, both temporal and spiritual; for the Divine Lord above would possess the land and rule over it. He whose Name is One and whose ways are those of righteousness and truth would have the regnancy. The great ones would be the servants of all, the true Kings of the East or the Divine Children whose diadem would be Christhood. The voice of oppression no more would be heard, for the deliverance of all the people would be accomplished. The claims of bondage and slavery would be broken, and all Souls would go forth into the glorious freedom which the Divine Love giveth, a freedom begotten of love and doing only the works of love. All Souls would walk in the true *Union of One Life*, however diversified its manifestations in their different spiritual states.

All Souls would live in the Light of the Divine, for the glory of the LORD would become the heritage of the Nations when everything crooked was made straight, everything broken and rough was made smooth, the low-lying valleys or conditions lifted up into the sunshine of the blessing of purity and goodness, and all the spiritual uplands and Divine Heights up which all life is to climb, made clear.

.   .   .   .

Such is the Western World as it should be as Christendom; and what it shall be when all the Churches have learnt the meaning of a Christian Church, and what it is to follow Christ. It is the Western World as it must become as the result of the forces which are now working within its Nations and Communities, causing Social and Religious upheavals, in the day when the Churches through being truly Christian are able to show forth the nature and meaning of the Redeemed Life through all their members living it, and to guide all seeking Souls into the true path of life along which alone Redemption is found and the Christ-vision beheld. It is what the Churches should have long ago made the Western World, and would have made it had they been truly Christian in character and service. But not knowing the meaning of the Redemption, they could not teach it; and not understanding the meaning of the Redeemed Life, they have not lived it. Therefore the people could not understand the meaning of purity in living.

Old things are now passing away; behold how all things are becoming new! The Churches are gradually changing. But even should they fail to find the meaning of the Redeemed Life and attain to it, yet shall the field of their operations be won unto the true life. For just as all the great movements for the upliftment of Humanity have begun outside the Churches, the new light has broken upon the Soul beyond their borders, and the Redeemed Life has become known and is practised by many outside their communions, so shall the world be won for GOD without the Ecclesiastical Priests and Schoolmen, and the agency of their materialized institutions and teachings. Some trust in Horses and some in Chariots—the powers of the mind and things material—but only to be disappointed; for the powers which are so born are incapable of uplifting, redeeming and illumining the Soul. Horses and Chariots are only useful when in the hands of those who are capable of rightly guiding them; and so are Churches and all their earthly powers. As mere Hierarchies they have won no world unto Christhood. As Priesthoods they have been powerless to portray Christ and present His vision to the world. As centres of Scholasticism they have failed to perceive the light which breaketh from the Eastern Heavens of the Divine, but have trusted solely to that light (which so frequently is only as the darkness) which cometh through history and tradition. As Spiritual Communions they have not known the *reality* of the things which they believed in, so could not make manifest their meaning.

But all things must and shall become new within them, and then may they indeed perform a beautiful ministry before the Lord as embodiments and manifestors of the Redeemed Life, and interpreters of His Love and Wisdom.

THE MAN OF NAZARETH

THE New Age is breaking amid great changes. The Religious World is electrically charged, and diverse forces are making themselves manifest. The elements are being moved, and the magnetic effects are heard of on every hand. The spirit of controversy is abroad, and it is breaking up ground that has long been fallow, and preparing the soil for the good seed. Old themes are discussed with new vigour, and points of view are as various as the interpretations which prevailed in the different ages.

"What think ye of Christ?" is being discussed with a fervour and an earnestness which can only bring good to the Churches. The old ways of answering the question are passing, though a few of the Scholars still cling to them. The magnetic attraction of Christ is great, though the real meaning of the attraction seems to be as yet little understood. The Master draws many to inquire who He is, but few find the true answer, *so lost are they in His personality.* They confound the CHRIST with the form through whom He is manifested, the Divine Logos with the man Jesus. Some think of Him as the Man of Nazareth, who attained the human stature which raised Him up as one who had reached Sonship to GOD; whilst others in varying ways view Him as the Son of GOD incarnate. By some He is loved as a hero and followed as a leader; by others

He is exalted to the seat of the Most High, and worshipped as only the Ever Blessed ONE should be worshipped. To the one class of adherents the real meaning of His Christhood is lost; by the other class the Christhood is materialized.

To behold Him only as Jesus of Nazareth, is to fail to understand His Christhood; to make His Christhood personal is not only to limit it, but to change its nature. For Christhood is not a personal thing in the sense in which we would think and speak of the person of a man. The Churches have been accustomed to think of the Divine and Ever Blessed ONE as a person, evidently not knowing that such an interpretation cannot be put upon the Divine Hypostasis. The Divine Hypostasis does not relate to the *persona* as of a man, but to the nature of the Divine. Even a man is only personal in relation to the form through which he makes manifest the real individuality; the latter is his own true Being, and that is entirely spiritual. How frequently the real man is not known through the personal. He is often better or worse than the manifestation—generally the former. But the Divine as such has no outward personal form. Whilst it may be helpful to many to think of GOD anthropomorphically, we must not forget that GOD is not a man.

That the Master was the Man Jesus surely none need doubt. By the man Jesus we mean perhaps more than at first appears. The very name is

fraught with profound meanings for us. The name
given Him in the Records was not His family name,
but the name which represented His mission. We
have a parallel case in Gautama having been named
the Buddha because of his mission. The Master
was called Jesus because He was the Saviour of
the people from their sins, so that the name implied
the mission. He had given to Him the name because
He was in the spiritual state which it represented.
He was to become the Saviour of the people because
He was in a state of Redemption, both knowing and
realizing the Redeemed Life. He was Jesus in
Himself as well as in His mission.

The mission of many men and women has been
greater and purer and nobler than they have been
in themselves: with Jesus it was otherwise. He
was what His mission represented. He knew from
experience the life unto which He called the people,
the life of the Redemption, the Redeemed Life. He
became their Saviour when they followed that life;
when they did not follow it, He could not save them.

That the following of Him was not meant personally, except that the personal life of the follower
was influenced unto Redemption, may be gathered
from several statements in the Records. There were
many who were said to be attached to Him who
followed Him whilst they thought He was going to
found a new kingdom, all of whom failed at the last
because their hopes were not realised. It was said

that the immediate disciples of Jesus found others who were not recognized as disciples casting out evil in His name, and that they requested Him to command them to follow with them; but that Jesus replied, "They who be not against us are for us."

Men and women have confused two distinct things, the personal form and the spiritual signification of the name. They have understood the term as personal and thus have missed its meaning. They have failed to discern that when the Master as the man Jesus invited men and women to follow Him, He was not asking for any personal attachment, but rather that they would follow the life implied in the name, the life which the Master beautifully illustrated. For the Redeemed Life made manifest by Him was that unto which He so earnestly counselled the people.

It has been one of the tragedies enacted in the history of the ages that the Records which purported to portray the Master as He was, should have so mispresented His portrait that, whilst He bears the name Jesus, He is not shown to embody the spiritual state which it signifies. He is made to eat flesh and drink wine, to encourage customs and habits barbarous and degrading, to give His name to a system represented by the Abattoirs and Shambles which speak of pain, suffering and anguish on the part of the Creatures, and inhumanity on the part of man.

That the writers of the Records did not know the

meaning of the term Jesus is evident from the presentation; or if they did, then they purposely misrepresented the life of the Master. Whichever it was, they have misled the whole of the Western World, and done despite unto the Master whose life was pure in all its ways, profoundly compassionate unto all Souls, and universally pitiful and gentle unto all the Creatures.

As the name Jesus signified the state of His own life and the redemptive mission on which He had come, so Christ signified also a state of consciousness which the Master had, and His Divine office of Interpreter of the Divine Love and Wisdom. He was Jesus Christ. It was neither a Christian name, as we designate the first name of anyone, nor a surname; it was a glorious state of inward Divine Realization which also fitted Him for the sublime mission. The term itself is significant. Just as Jesus meant that the Master was a Saviour of men, so Christ meant that He was the vehicle of the Logos, the ADONAI, the ever blessed Son of the Eternal ONE. *The Christ* was the Anointed One. To be anointed is to be Illumined from the Divine. To be illumined is to know the Divine through inward realization, to have the perfect consciousness of the Divine Presence dwelling within the Sanctuary of Being.

It was thus with the Master. He was Jesus Christ, the anointed or Illumined One from the Divine Kingdom. He was the vehicle of the Logos who is ever in the bosom of the FATHER-MOTHER, and who was with Him and in Him. He was therefore able to speak as one who knew the Divine Mystery of Being and who was in perfect harmony with the life and purpose of that Most Blessed ONE. His Saviourhood was crowned with Christhood. He was the Redeemer of men through making manifest the Redeemed Life that they might follow it. He was Christ or the Interpreter of the Divine Love and Wisdom, which He showed forth in the Teachings that He gave to the inner group of the disciples. As Jesus He made plain for all the life that was to be lived; as Christ He revealed the attainment of the Crown of Life as the outcome of the Redemption. As Jesus He taught men how to make their lives pure on all its planes; as Christ He taught Souls how to realise the Divine love within themselves, and come into the beautiful consciousness of the Divine Presence within the Sanctuary of Being. As Jesus He called all unto the life of Self-denial and Self-sacrifice; as Christ He constrained Souls to give themselves in beautiful Abandonment to the Divine. The one was the Office of the Redeemer; the other was the Office of the Interpreter of the Divine. Both were divinely appointed; and both were Offices of the Cross.

His Christhood has been as little understood as His Office of Redeemer. The Records that failed to show how He lived the Life of the Redemption to save men, confused His Christhood, and gave a false vision of it unto all who trusted in these Records.

But there is yet one other title which was given unto the Master by the writers of the Records, which likewise was applied to Him personally, but which was wholly Divine in its significance. He was also spoken of as the LORD. In every instance in which it is made use of, the designation is applied to the man. It is the man who is spoken of as Divine. The inner significance of the appellation is thus entirely lost, whilst the mere form through whom the Divine has been manifested is exalted to the Divine Kingdom and crowned Deity. For the term LORD as applied to the Master implies Deific Regnance and speaks of the ruling power of the Divine Love. It speaks of the Christhood of the Master as having been crowned with the ruling power implied in the title of LORD. And in doing that it signifies that just as the Master's Life and Office of the Redeemer was crowned with the Christhood Estate, so His Christhood was the outcome of the Divine Overshadowing.

There is but one LORD, as the Blessed Master taught, and HIS Name is ONE. HE alone is the LORD of the Heavens and the Earth. HE alone is the Ruler in High Places, the spiritual and Divine realms. HE is the ADONAI, the ever Blessed Son of GOD. HE alone is KING of Kings and LORD of Lords.

But HE is not personal, though HE makes manifest the Divine within the Soul who has attained

Christhood. When HE is present, the Fear or Divine Awe of the LORD fills all Souls. Those who are disciples indeed of the Christhood require not to ask who it is, knowing that it is the LORD. It was not concerning the personal Jesus that the disciples made the inquiry, for they knew Him well. His form and ways were familiar to them. But there were times when the conditions were such that they were filled with wonder and awe, and made inquiry one of another as to the meaning of them, until they came to the blessed knowledge that it was the approach of the LORD, the overshadowing of the Divine Love.

The writers of the Records were unable to distinguish between personal and Divine things, so they mixed them. They did not understand the vehicle nature of the personal life, and naturally applied all the beautiful terms to that life. They first gave the personal the title of Jesus, then Christ, and then the LORD, and so they made the man the LORD Christ Jesus. They failed to perceive the significance of the titles as the Divine Presence, the Soul crowned with the fulness of that Presence through Christhood, and the Life of the Redemption made manifest. They beheld not how the terms expressed the way in which the Ever Blessed ONE communicated direct with the Human Kingdom as the LORD Christ Jesus; nor how they showed forth the ascent of the Soul to the Divine Kingdom when

the Divine Love alone rules throughout the whole
Being, as Jesus, Christ, and our LORD.

And thus did they crown their other mistakes by
presenting the man as the Divine LORD, the One to
be adored and worshipped. Thus did they lead the
whole Western World into another form of idolatry.

.   .   .   .

But the day has dawned wherein those most
grievous mistakes shall be rectified. The Temple
of the Christhood that was pulled down through
the misrepresentation, is once more to be restored.
The miraging mists are being blown away, and
the true Vision in its full resplendence is to be
revealed. And in it shall all who are able to
understand, behold the Glory of the LORD.

THE VISION OF THE LORD

I saw the Lord.
He stood before me on the shores
Of Sacred Galilee, whose calm, clear waters could
Reflect the glory of the Heavens by which they were
O'ershadowed, and the Hills and Mountains which rose
Peak above peak, those Uplands of the Soul, the home
Of Angels, the Heights Divine whence streameth far God's
Glory in unclouded day, wondrous, unspeakable.

At first I knew Him not, so clouded was my
Vision; for sorrow had laid her heavy hand upon
Me, and deep grief had struck its roots into my life.
For I had sought my Lord with great desire and tear-
Stained countenance and anguishing of Soul, yet found
Him not; the Night had closed about me, and the Stars
Were lost amid the darkness, those Angelic Lamps
Dependent from the Heavens, that I could not find
My way back to the land of Life Immortal, that
Land of pure delight and joy unspeakable, where
Saints dwell and evil is unknown, the land whose
Pastures are God's Wisdom rich and full, whose rivers
Flow still, calm, and deep, bearing Life's Waters for the
Soul, rivers of Love Celestial and Divine.

But when I saw His form, His well-known Countenance,
Radiant with Light ineffable which made the
Darkness fade and brought in day, His vesture seamless,
Pure, glorious, then knew I that it was the Lord.

And when I heard His voice, so full of gentleness
(So tender were His words), my sorrow was no more
With me, nor the deep grief which pulsed through my veins,
Nor anguish overwhelming at my loss, but in
Their stead came peace and joy and comfort such as He
Alone could give my Soul.
"As ye have naught to eat,
Come dine with Me: Take ye this Bread of Life and be
Ye nourished, this Mystery of Love strengthening
And fitting you to bear your Cross, your burden, through
The Via Dolorosa unto Calvary's Hill,
The Pathway of the Christs, the Sons of God who bear
The burden of the world unto Redemption, and
Yield themselves in Service to their Lord, sublimely.

Lo, I am with you alway, e'en when the shadows
Fall as when the light is full, to guide you.
I will never leave you, nor forsake my Temple
Wherein I love to dwell in commune with the Soul."

Thus spake He; and there came upon me His own Holy
Breath which filled me with His Peace, and made me joyous,
And caused the fire to burn upon my Altar night and day,
And lit my lamp with His own glorious Light.

O Blessed Vision of my Soul! My mind is Galilee,
And there upon its shores my Lord doth walk.

A VISION OF THE MASTER.

There came to me a vision in the Night of this
World's travail, in which I saw the Master as He
Was when Nazareth was His home in Galilee.
And I must tell that vision unto you to show
How beautiful was His life, how pure in all its
Spheres. He knew no wrong nor in His ways did evil;
He loved all Souls; the Creatures He did shield from those
Who would oppress them; Compassion flowed in fullness
Unto all, and bore upon its crest unfailing
Pity, which passed to the remotest states of life
Finding the wounded ones to touch and heal them.

No Creature suffered from His look, His word, His deed;
No life was sacrificed to meet His earthly wants;
His lips were stainless, free from the darkening,
Polluting sin of shedding blood. All Life to Him
Was sacred. His pathway saw no bloodmarks where He
Trod, which spake of mangled forms and anguish-cries of
Helpless victims within the awful Abattoirs:

He was a Man complete, holy and true, whose
Vestures were the garments of pure life; a Man
Beneficent, upon whose brow there sat that crown
Which good men fain would merit—the Crown of Good,
Image of the Gods, resplendent with a love
God-born, boundless, free for all, knowing no limits
In its giving, nor recognizing any.

To Him
All Souls were dear as unto God; no Human kind
Nor Creature, howsoe'er remote, He passed by
Unheeded, but gave His Benison of healing
Love, and called all Souls to follow in His Way,
The Way of Life Redeemed from bondage, sin and woe;
The Soul upraised, from evil freed, and sphered in love;
The Life of Self-denial that would scorn to make
A Creature suffer pain, or have its days cut short
To minister to desire; the Life that seeks
No pleasure in this world born of desire, but only
That of sacrifice, full beautiful, Divine, that
Gives out from its own in service born of love.

Such was my vision; now may ye behold the Man
Whose way was narrow, but which led to Life.

THE VISION OF CHRISTHOOD

I saw the Heavenly Christ: Grace from His lips did flow
And find its utterance in the Master's life; in Him
The Holy Wisdom of the Gods dwelt as Treasure
Precious in a treasure-house, and found an outlet
In His gracious words and deeds. These were as gems
Whose facets to illumine Souls threw out the
Radiance of the Gods, Wisdom of Heaven and
Love Divine, as light refracted, beautiful and
Glorious to behold, full of the images
Of things Divine, the secrets of the Gods.
His words were fraught with Life Immortal, Life
For all souls whose cherished aim it is to know
The Christhood, that Estate whose riches are so great
That they endow the Soul with wealth whose increase is
Of God, wealth which never makes impoverishment,
Nor tarnishes, nor gives those cankering cares which
Follow earthly gain, but riches great and holy,
Knowledge and Love Eternal, Wisdom Divine, Light
Whose glory is the reflex of the Lord, and Royal
Diadem, crown of the Sons of God. Upon the
Master's brow there sat that royal dignity, emblem divine
Of one who had been named Son of God and sent
Forth from the Heavenly Kingdom by Him the Hebrews
Knew as Adonai, the Lord of Life, the Manifest
Of Him no mortal eye hath seen, the Invisible
And Ever Blessed One. Within the Christ there burned
The sacred Fires kindled by Elohim, the Seven
Spirits majestic from the throne of the Eternal,
Those sacred Spirits whom God giveth unto all

Who know His Fear, the Holy Awe, in Christhood;
And these shone forth the Light of the Eternal Love
(Even as the Sun pours out his glory during day)
To shine upon man's pathway leading him to Heaven,
That path by which all Souls must gain the goal,
Rising above things earthly to find their fullness
In the Life and Love Eternal; Such was the Christ.
Shall we not seek to follow Him, to share His Cup,
His baptism and His Service? To know Denial, Sacrifice,
Abandonment, perfect, complete, unto the will of
Heaven? To follow on from Sphere to Sphere in service,
Glorious in nature, life-redeeming, until we too
Are crowned Sons of God? For such is Christhood.

The Order of the Cross

SPIRITUAL
AIMS AND IDEALS

THE Order is an informal Brother-
hood and Fellowship, having for
its service in life the cultivation of
the Spirit of Love towards all Souls:
Helping the weak and defending the
defenceless and oppressed ; Abstaining
from hurting the creatures, eschewing
bloodshed and flesh eating, and living
upon the pure foods so abundantly
provided by nature ; Walking in the
Mystic Way of Life, whose Path leads
to the realization of the Christhood ;
And sending forth the Mystic Teachings
unto all who may be able to receive
them — those sacred interpretations
of the Soul, the Christhood, and
the Divine Love and Wisdom, for
which the Order of the Cross stands.

SYNOPSIS OF MAIN PUBLICATIONS

THE MASTER sets forth the Inner Meanings of the Master's Teachings and gives a true picture of Him as He was in His Life, public and private. The Birth Stories and the Allegories of the Soul are revealed in their true setting; with the Teachings on the profound Mystery of the Sin-offering, and the Allegories of the Soul's Awakening.

THE LOGIA contains the chief utterances of the Master, in the form in which they were spoken by Him. Here they are restored, including the real Mystic Sayings, found in the Synoptic Records, the Gnostic Record, the Pauline Letters, and the Apocalypse, containing remarkable histories of the Soul, the Planet, the Ancient Christhood Order, and the Oblation or Sin-offering.

LIFE'S MYSTERIES UNVEILED gives the Path of Discipleship and Aids to the Path of the Realization. It includes definitions of terms in their relation to these Teachings and many answers to questions asked at Healing and other Meetings. The principal theme of the volume is Initiations of the Soul.

THE DIVINE RENAISSANCE, Vol. I. i. The Message. The Divine Adept. The Superstructure of Man. ii. The Eternal Mystery. A Divine Apologia. The Seat of Authority. iii. The Path of the Recovery. The Redemption. The Divine Purpose of the Oblation. The Mass and the Oblation. Altars and Sacrifices. The Flame before the Altar.

THE DIVINE RENAISSANCE, Vol. II. i. Unto the Great Silence. Science and Religion. The Angelic Realms. Corpus Christi. The Sabbath of the Lord. ii. Beginnings of Historical Christianity. Pentecost. The Advent of Paul. The Stone the Builders Rejected. The Church of the Living Christ. The Seven Sacraments. iii. A Renascent Redemption. The Seven Thunders. The Healer, Manifestor, Redeemer. The Obedience of Christ. Our Lord and Our Lady. The Three Altars. iv. A Divine Oratorio. The Ministry of the Gods. The Divine Government. The Cosmic Consciousness. The Regnancy of Christ.

THE MESSAGE OF EZEKIEL. *A COSMIC DRAMA.* The Office of a Prophet. The Purport of the Book. The Divine World Unveiled. The Distinction given to Israel. The Mystery of Tyre and Zidon. The Pharaoh of Egypt. The Arising of Israel. The *Logia* of the Prophet Ezekiel: with extensive Notes to the *Logia*. *The Logia of Israel.* Vol. I.

THE MYSTERY OF THE LIGHT WITHIN US. *With* 17 *coloured plates by Amy Wright Todd Ferrier.* i. The Luminous Cross and the Cross of the Elohim. ii. The Spectra of Souls and Stars. The Solar Fashion. iii. Auric Glimpses of the Master. iv. Celestial and Divine Estates. v. A Holy Convocation. Jacob's Ladder. The Adamic Race. The Secrets of God. The Girdle. The Blessing of Israel. A Divine Rhapsody.

ISAIAH. *A COSMIC AND MESSIANIC DRAMA.* i. The Unity of Divine Revelation. ii. The Prophecy. iii. The Word of the Lord. iv. A Divine Drama. v. The Mystery of the Sin-offering. vi. A Momentous Promise. vii. The Triumph of Adonai. viii. The Drama of Israel. ix. The Sign of the Cross. x. The Daysman of Israel. xi. The Appointed Redeemer. xii. The Five Cities of Egypt. xiii. The City of the Sun. xiv. The *Logia* of the Prophet Isaiah: with extensive Notes. *The Logia of Israel.* Vol. II.

PUBLICATIONS

By the REV. J. TODD FERRIER:

THE MASTER: *His Life and Teachings*	Large Crown 8vo		624 pp.
THE LOGIA: *or Sayings of The Master*	,, ,,	,,	436 pp.
LIFE'S MYSTERIES UNVEILED	,, ,,	,,	480 pp.
THE DIVINE RENAISSANCE, Vol. I	,, ,,	,,	402 pp.
THE DIVINE RENAISSANCE, Vol. II	,, ,,	,,	560 pp.
THE MESSAGE OF EZEKIEL: *A Cosmic Drama*	,, ,,	,,	280 pp.
THE MESSAGE OF ISAIAH: *A Cosmic and Messianic Drama*	,, ,,	,,	436 pp.

THE MYSTERY OF THE LIGHT WITHIN US

With 17 plates. Large Crown 4to 240 pp.

THE HERALD OF THE CROSS (Bound volumes)

Vols. VIII upwards Large Crown 8vo

HANDBOOK OF EXTRACTS of the Teachings of The Order of the Cross, from the Writings of the Rev. J. Todd Ferrier.

Vol. I: Extracts A to D; Vol. II: Extracts E to J. Demy 8vo

Further volumes in preparation.

LETTERS TO THE CHILDREN ,, ,, 238 pp.

SMALLER BOOKS (Paper Bound)

THE MYSTERY OF THE CITY UPON SEVEN HILLS	Demy 8vo		80 pp.
GREAT RECOVERIES	,,	,,	80 pp.
THE FESTIVAL OF THE MASS OF ISRAEL	,,	,,	72 pp.
THE STORY OF THE SHEPHERDS OF BETHLEHEM	,,	,,	72 pp.
SUBLIME AFFIRMATIONS	,,	,,	64 pp.
WHAT IS A CHRISTIAN?	,,	,,	64 pp.
THE EVANGEL OF ST. JOHN	,,	,,	40 pp.
THE GREAT TRIBULATION . THE WORK	,,	,,	40 pp.
THE CHRIST FESTIVAL . THE WAYS OF GOD AND THE WAYS OF MEN	,,	,,	36 pp.
THE CROSS OF A CHRIST . THE RESURRECTION LIFE	,,	,,	36 pp.
THE CONTINUITY OF CONSCIOUSNESS	,,	,,	28 pp.
IF CHRIST CAME BACK?	,,	,,	24 pp.
THE LIFE IMMORTAL	,,	,,	20 pp.
THE ORDER OF THE CROSS	,,	,,	16 pp.
THE MESSAGE AND THE WORK	,,	,,	12 pp.
THE INNER MEANING OF THE FOOD REFORM MOVEMENT	,,	,,	8 pp.
ON BEHALF OF THE CREATURES	Crown 8vo		128 pp.
THOUGHTS FOR THE DAY	,,	,,	52 pp.
THE SECOND COMING OF CHRIST	,,	,,	48 pp.
THE ABRAHAMIC STORY	,,	,,	20 pp.

By E. MARY GORDON KEMMIS:

THE "GREATER WORKS" (Cloth bound) Crown 8vo 64 pp.

FOR USE IN WORSHIP

PSALMS AND CANTICLES FOR WORSHIP (Paper or Cloth bound)	Demy 8vo		96 pp.
HYMNS FOR WORSHIP WITH TUNES	,,	,,	256 pp.

THE HERALD OF THE CROSS

Vols. I to VII (published 1905-11) are now out of print. Vols. VIII (1934) to XXI (six issues a year) and Vols. XXII upwards (four issues a year) are available separately, paper bound, in limited quantities. (Vols. VIII to XVII, No. 4, edited by the Rev. J. Todd Ferrier: subsequent issues edited according to his instructions.)

All prices on Application

Please address all communications regarding Literature, and make remittances payable, to THE LITERATURE SECRETARY, THE ORDER OF THE CROSS, 10 DE VERE GARDENS, LONDON, W.8.

Loan copies of any of the publications may be applied for to THE LIBRARIAN.

MEETINGS

Regular meetings are held, at which all seekers after the Divine way of life are welcome, in the Sanctuary at the Headquarters of the Order of the Cross, as below, every Sunday at 11 a.m. and Wednesday at 7 p.m. throughout the year (except during the Summer Vacation); and there are Groups or Reading Circles for the study of the Teachings at:—

Aberdeen; Belfast; Birmingham; Bournemouth and Christchurch; Bradford; Brighton; Bristol; Cardiff; Colchester; Dundee; Edinburgh; Glasgow; Gloucester; Guildford; Inverness; Leicester; Leigh-on-Sea; Letchworth; Liverpool; Manchester; Newport, Mon; Nottingham; Reading; Sheffield; Stockton-on-Tees; Stratford-on-Avon; Sunderland; Tyneside; and also in the London area, at Croydon; Epping Forest; Hampstead; Kensington Gardens; Kew Gardens; Pinner, Middlesex; Westbourne; Woodford, Essex. Also at Melbourne, Australia; Auckland, Christchurch, New Zealand; Los Angeles, Salt Lake City, San Francisco, U.S.A.; Paris, France.

COMMUNICATIONS

Communications regarding the Literature of the Order should be addressed, and remittances made payable to, " The Literature Secretary," at the Headquarters.

Further information concerning the Order of the Cross and its activities will be given gladly to any inquirer, on application to:

THE SECRETARY

THE ORDER OF THE CROSS
10 DE VERE GARDENS, KENSINGTON,
LONDON, W.8